Yvonne Rainer

Poems

Poems
Yvonne Rainer

Second printing

Published by
Badlands Unlimited
P.O. Box 151
New York, NY 10002
Email: operator@badlandsunlimited.com
URL: www.badlandsunlimited.com

Enhanced e-book with multimedia content available on Apple iBooks, Amazon Kindle, and other e-readers. For more information, visit www.badlandsunlimited.com

Front cover: Joel Reynolds and Yvonne Rainer during *Assisted Living: Good Sports 2* at Baryshnikov Arts Center, New York, March 2011. Back cover: set of *Assisted Living: Good Sports 2*. Photos by Mathieu Malouf

Book design by Paul Chan
E-book design by Ian Cheng
Special thanks to Alexandra Tuttle and Greene Naftali Gallery, Nickolas Calabrese, Sean Wehle, and Brook Wilensky-Lanford

ISBN: 978-1-936440-10-8
E-book ISBN: 978-1-936440-11-5

Generated in the United States of America

Printed in the United States of America on acid-free paper

www.badlandsunlimited.com

For Martha Gever

CONTENTS

ILLUSTRATIONS

KEEP MOVING:
THE POEMS OF YVONNE RAINER

Tim Griffin

A strong correspondence between dance and poetry was established more than a century ago, when Stéphane Mallarmé, surveying the discipline of ballet in 1886, famously asserted that a dancer does not really dance, but rather "suggest[s], through the miracle of bends and leaps, a kind of corporal writing: ... a poem independent of any scribal apparatus." Yet by now this dialogue of movement and text cannot be seen through the restrictive prisms of dance and poetry alone. Mallarmé's spatialization of language would, for example, go on to underpin various artists' efforts during the 1960s to expand linguistic models into cultural and institutional registers. If a word becomes meaningful only in relation to the organization of surrounding words, their logic goes, so any self-reflexive artistic endeavor should extend beyond its literal borders to engage with the structures of the media, disciplines, and social conventions of the world around it in order for the work to find its true shape. Moreover, Mallarmé's analyses of dance onstage have since migrated to elementary movement through space, as when Michel de Certeau, in *The Practice of Everyday Life*, writes of "poetic walking," whereby a pedestrian introduces skips and jumps into the logic of urban architectures and their intended uses. Even daily actions, in other words, entail a kind of grammar. And, as the body in motion produces new and other encounters, the subject can act at once as a kind of reader and writer of her own experience. In fact—and admittedly at the risk of Francophilia here—it is in this way that philosopher Jacques Ranciére understands Mallarmé's original assertion regarding dance and poetry: as a marvelous expression of the in-between, a slippage in perception from one surface to another, whether page, dance floor, canvas, or musical score. It is in negotiating the area between such objects and abstract organizational principles—in the everyday, in other words—that life can be lived, poetically. Or, more aptly said, it is in this way that life is finally set in motion.

From the very beginning of Yvonne Rainer's present volume of poems—her first, written during the late 1990s and early 2000s—readers will be tempted to consider the act of writing within such a historical frame (expanding that frame as well to accommodate Rainer's political and social engagements, familiar to anyone acquainted with her other work). For example, in "1977," the poem with which the book opens, Rainer's composition seems closely attuned to her choreography, with phrases in language resembling those in dance. Here a simple, steady cadence provides procedural measure for simple, pared-down words, with enjambments introducing (inducing?) plain yet elegant turns that move the eyes forward, across, and down the page. One thing follows the next; and yet one move always implies another to come, so that the subject herself is always in transition. Rainer's careful delineation of temporality, it seems, only makes the actions filling her outline more palpable. Even thematically, there is continuous motion, whether from sleeping to waking state, from winter to just-perceived spring at the poem's conclusion, propelled by Rainer's uncoiling phrase, "When next I noticed…." All the more clear in this regard is "Trio A," which nearly renders corporal writing actual on the writing plane, as Rainer writes: When it's right / nothing's like it…

    not a flicker

    of doubt

    mars the flow

    of arm

    into hip

    into knee

    into floor

If Rainer once remarked that she wished to treat the body as just another object, unadorned and not stylized—like a mattress— here she gives equal weight, in line following line, to knee, hip, and floor. Each figure leads to the next in a list that continues (with nothing "impeding / the forward momentum") to the poem's final observation that "the weight of the body / is material proof that air is matter / and mind's married to muscle." The intellect is always of a piece with the physical realm.

Perhaps it's a similar sense of language made physical—of poems themselves as corporal forms, creating and occupying a kind of mental space even while residing as ink on the page—that is most remarkable about Rainer's poetry. Notably in this regard, Rancière will also remark that Mallarmé, writing about dance, is a poet of the "event." That is, the poet creates situations in which words and actions can actually take place, giving them a space in which they are made legible for the mind's eye, and given meaning. Such rendering of scenes is also important in Rainer's poems, and frequently appear in short narratives—as when she describes encounters in the post office, or on the R train subway platform. On these occasions one might well recall that Rainer spent some of her youth in San Francisco, frequenting the City Lights bookstore and even attending the first reading of "Howl." Indeed, whatever else her poems do, they obtain here a first-person, even brute beatnicity when Rainer barks a loud answer—"ahead of my brain"—to someone asking where Grand Central Station is; or when, recalling a gathering of artists of her generation, she wryly writes, "We're all here together / minus kidneys and breasts." These moments, summoning the likes of Lawrence Ferlinghetti, are almost always soon complemented by episodes of elegiac materialism, as when Rainer makes the blunt observation that "my hamstring hurts" in the back of a cab in the otherwise-cinematic summer scene of "Hot Dusk"; when, with prose-like facticity, she eggs on a companion to express her feelings in "I Love You"; or when Rainer's cadence reaches an exuberant double-time toward the end of "Orgasms."

Yet a subtler legibility is also at work here, I think, in that the episodic, almost notational quality of each individual poem suggests the workings of mnemonic devices. More specifically, as Rainer's different verses prompt a sense of space and physical movement—with enjambments making physical turns in lettering, and with scenes described turned over in the mind— for me they recall the techniques of lecturers who cue passages from speeches to different objects in the room. Remembering and walking are one. (While speaking publicly, and as early as in ancient Rome or Baroque-period France, one might think of architectural spaces, using different objects and images in this mental picture as a prompt for each new phrase or passage.) Of course, as a dancer and choreographer, Rainer would naturally find memory contained in physical form, or in practice. Just as each movement of the body contains within it the next movement, so language must create a space for movement in order to allow for memory. As if to tip her hand to the reader, Rainer includes the poem "Indices," in which she "patrol[s] this space" containing all the markers of others' missing presence; it is the area around that reveals the absence as, for instance, "The impression of your head / etches the pillow." Also interspersed among Rainer's words are many clippings and photographs—markers and prompts—from a picture of herself wearing a pot lid in the kitchen, to one of Merce Cunningham dancing, and another of Carles Puyol dramatically

5

surrounded by his teammates (as if composed by Delacroix) after a World Cup goal. But here again, keepsakes: pictures with meaning only in space, by the desk, on the fridge, in the home.

Immediately following that last image of Puyol, in the poem "Seville next day," are Rainer's most telling lines:

> The effort of parsing memory
>
> into logic
>
> say 25 years or more
>
> giving way

Lines on the page give shape to the past, allowing it to exist, to be approached, to come closer. But, for Rainer, this happens only while giving herself continuous instruction, as in the final words of "Walking in the City": Keep moving.

•

Tim Griffin is a poet, critic, and director and chief curator at The Kitchen.

1977

I dreamed of bodies burning at the edges
When I awoke my belly was cold as an abandoned stove
The streets were cleared, trees bent
The air so still, as though just inhaled
When next I noticed it was spring

Socrates NYC

"Are you looking for someone?"
I've eaten my single poached
in a cup
wheat down
dry
Where is she?
Who is she?

Each woman
stymies my scrutiny
clothes wrong
age wrong
expression wrong
bearing wrong

The waitress all wrong
too old for the work
too bent for the work
too tired for the work
too long suffering
for the goddamned work
written all over her

I start to leave
my rescuer arrives
Ah, now there are two of us
to focus on me

Socrates January 27, 1999
Tuesday morning

Waiting again
single poached etc.
He's the one who changed the date
one irascibility
assuages another
he arrives
older
larger
more important

we move through those thickets
very fast these days
memory clogs
his easy overs

Bilbao

Bilbao Bilbao
She yawns
(I move backwards)
swallows hard against
her air-locked ears

more searching for food
apparitions outside a bar
direct descendants from the
Some forget the war
They wear their institutional red cotton jackets
a reproachful reminder
in perfect English:
"I'm total Basque
they made us get out"
like South Africa
everyone has a story
as they point you to food
We ate contentiously
our stories paling

En route Madrid-NY 1-10-99

Mack Sennett flight attendants
recall the restaurant in Seville
One of us never did get her meal
the olives sufficed
pungent, acrid, oily, cloying
In unaccustomed dependence
we balked and pleasured

Seville

What we saw
in passing what
we didn't
avoiding what we couldn't

a Carmen's coil
wrapped unwrapping
an image revoked
a dream imagined

The magistrate's palace
its muffled stones
mispoken documents
empirical reach
labors uncounted
a hole to heaven
my colón unattended
(his bones long dispersed
their claims duly filed)

lost doggy
cats in the sun
rumbling gut
No matter what arrests the eye
panty liner
travel broadens
"That's what it's all about"
she said in front of
the four-star hotel
honing not having
pretending not to want

men middle-aged
in suits
selling lottery tickets

When her ship comes in
a dream of empire
behind regrets
not enough sex

betrayals
expulsions
populations cleansed
(unhappy word)
the stones wailed
as we trod by the hundreds
each step a wish
the pilgrim's dilemma

at night we return
the Carmen's coil
the arrest
the worm unturned

We saw no squalor

Goal PH "directs"

Carles Puyol, second from right, nearly disappeared in the celebration after his goal gave Spain the lead.

MATT DUNHAM/ASSOCIATED

Patient and R

Seville next day

The UN grapples
while the winter sun
angles acutely
in the thronging passage
four musicians
in sweaters
pushing 45
play Mozart
their concentration
just this side
of tears

The effort of parsing memory
into logic
say 25 years or more
giving way

RainerO in the Post Office

They raised the rates
one window closes
leaving two
for fifty people
"Better off dead"
the wizened guy behind me
doesn't respect my personal space
One voice brazens
and facilitates
shortens the line
sends our George Washingtons
into oblivion
"Are you sure she works here?"
"She'd better work here
I have a gun"

Hours pass

"Better Off Dead"
reads my envelopes
"Are you French?"
my no-o-o must sound surly
"All right, all right, all right"
before I can say Italian
and recover the o

Hours pass

"GRAND CENTRAL STATION IS AT 42ND AND WHAT?!"
"PARK!" barks my mouth
ahead of my brain

O the ennui

I Love You

Not how to say it
When
like writing a poem
pay attention
to shifts of wind
opportunity
crack in the door

fortifications
no longer needed
at least for the moment
what a relief
only then
C'mon
say it

Orgasms

Are we going to do it?
the air is cleared
How do you feel about it?
it's hard to remember
so much work

The prologue goes smoothly
ablutions
giggles
caresses
whoops
come back

Meet the occasion
I ditch all the
residues, tatters, tangents, smarts
flail through the skeins
the needles fall away
and lo and behold
I'm loose as a goose
the meshes of her voice
tipping me over
each edge receding
no end in sight

Domesticity

Economy of scarcity
scares off
I care for you
(and know you care for me)

How much more satisfying
to feed grievances
stave off longing
stay hungry

economy of scarcity
promises vindication
delivers famine

the vacuum cleaner
wins the day

Two Homes
Waiting for take-off at Laguardia

What's left to beef about?
the fat woman across the aisle
is pleased with her Statue of Liberty
for eighteen dollars

no more bargains
for me
in the Presidents' Day Sale
of social protest

I must go home again
earlier battles beckon

The Faculty Club

Unexpectedly
the faculty club respite
offers a view
stock still
it stands
on the edge of the pond

cards slap the table
"Ah yeh
I'm going to the bottom
You're cutting
Ha!
Can't do anything now"

it hasn't stirred
eyes to the page
will the blue heron. . .
"I said hearts once"
the ducks parade
in the heart of academe

Now the light
yellows
the sunny rain
slackens
the ducks skid past
the unflappable heron

the rain returns

the ducks startle up
the heron remains

eyes to the page
it's gone

Waiting for Lives of Performers to end at Marymount
College NYC

Back in my skin
flayed's not the word
ten days of battened hatches
it would've taken a typhoon
to make me laugh
ORDER was the name of things
overlording disarray
the stuff of family
kept in check
What erupts
is never what matters
What matters
is always out of reach
their sentiment
my bathos
brother's agonies
my mask
his amnesias
my dismay

my never and always
my melodrama

John Bayley's Italics (Elegy for Iris) Victoria, B.C.

A hot day
under the oak
We trailed slowly
up Fritz's hill
it was 1950
I had no illusions
or, better, expectations
Rivers featured
and steep ravines
I never missed Iris
or Eunice Rice
The house and premises
allowed her seduction
In some way
so normal
for those times
In 1994
by then forgotten
Didn't Margaret Thatcher
ever go home
The horrid wish
the mean rage
Iris surprised me
Ivan remembered
When are we going
my imminent homecoming
Moving from stage
to mythic return
The agony

unspoken
I am continually
reminded
Nightmare recollection
decease in the napkin rings
Anger sometimes seems
so inappropriate
I always liked
that moment's memory
As I am sitting
her glowing warmth
That Christmas business
had nothing to do with it

Numbers

Joe designed a house
in the country
on 5 acres

I designed my life
in art
nearing 65

Joe does my taxes
in his friend's dingy apartment
once a year

I know Joe better
than all those strangers
one for seven years

and I don't own
a single house

August 2, 1999

"I went out there to see her
and she died"
that was that
reported deaths can be so flat
death fixes taxes
and small dependencies
Joe's wife Rita
never could drive
to that house
in the country

I miss him even
before taxes

Sun. March 28, 1999

She cancels herself
like a postal clerk
stamps each audacious
act of intellection
each move a dance
of retraction
and gainsaying
that lays her low
with indecision
and rage

Sat. April 3, 1999

All unaware
at the red door
my throat disgorges
memory's groan
etching the moment

her life foreclosed
I bought her
green dumplings
someone passing might think
"one of those crones"
who—me?
more like a multiple
risible and wrung

The Animals

Her love of cats
the danger of it
this placid beast
astride her ribs
conjoining bodies
the trouble with his is
he won't move it
her stretching dislodges
him once too often
The leopard attacks
She parries and blocks
under her thumb
the cheetah dissembles
biding his time
then straight for the face
this time he means it
She is the stronger
and don't you forget it
the fight to the finish
ends in the closet
her arm is a mess
he couldn't care less

34

Jealousy

I dance at his memorial
Does imagining him dead
enclose a wish
replace desire?
It's hard to believe
I want his shoes
I want what I had
everything after
a measly substitute
boneless proxy

youth?
applause?
camaraderie?
is it hubris
that pushes me back
into such jeopardy?
I sit obsessed
in astounded regression
this twaddle about risk
they don't know the half of it
those cultural bureaucrats

Mobilization

Marshaling my resources
I retreat from the throng
the object of adulation
now my objective
a beeline beckons
the mission is clear:
traverse this plane
do not pass go
keep your blindered gaze
on that golden door
Hey! the room's empty
I've walked right past him
sheepish now
I reconnoiter
embrace, banter
wag my tail

Call out the troops
to step off the curb
one false move
and the jig is up

Driving in Jo'berg, Oct. 1998

We stop at the light
his stories accelerate

this is where they car-jack

now with no roadblocks
the poor are impatient

He had ridden out his censure
in academic safety
before apartheid struggles
became jitney wars

the light turns green

nothing impedes us
neither the midnight streets
shrouding their secrets
nor the steel-gated villas
stilling their shudders

Friendship

The quiet unnerves me

(Madame de
caught offguard
by love's incursion)

nature rushes in
where this human rashly treads
and five old friends
after thirty years
of hiatuses
harnessed longing
revised reprises

perform the old tactics
with new-found pleasure

Hot Dusk

In the dwindling light
a thousand AC's
give up the ghost

The taxi's interior
dimly glows
like that Hopper diner

the cabby
turns
to return my gaze

his brown skin
glistens

my hamstring hurts

Trio A

When it's right
nothing's like it
the pieces fall
into place
not a flicker
of doubt
mars the flow
of arm
into hip
into knee
into floor
then midsection
hollowed in triumph
the whole apparatus
its discrete minds
not impeding
the forward momentum
of practice
of object
no ritual here
the weight of the body
is material proof
that air is matter
and mind's married to muscle

Take the R train

Southbound
on the R platform
the Chinese baritone
plays his Yamaha keyboard
and sings O Sole Mio

Southbound
on the R platform
I float a dollar
into his hat
and ask him
"What's that from?"

Smiling shyly
on the R platform
almost no English
"Italian folk song
O Sole Mio"
"my father. . ."

before the words are out
"...used to sing it"
on the R platform
the song
my father used to sing
crashes into the station

"Come un sogno d'oro"
like a golden dream
on the R platform

The Words

There are certain words
that elicit mawkish sighs
or at least a gulp
in some cerebral throats
like "my father"
(forget mother)
or   cobblestone
(forget Kosovo)
or   raging hormones
(forget East Timor)
or   interpellate
(forget food stamps)
in any case
the simple trick
is not to pause
but shun the corpse
and—nimble-witted—
outflank the rollicking
nightly news

Saga

I.
He was fond of saying
"She adores me
thinks I'm great"
toward the end
I knew better
sadly, or fortunately
he didn't
guilt notwithstanding
why face the truth
unless you have to

Toward the end
she shrilled
"HE NEEDS HELP!"
words breaking breath
systems winding down
and then: "See you later,
alligator"

let him go
(to whatever hell)
take me, Morpheus
down down down
and out the winder
Ma. MA!
organ grinder
does your mother know you're out
with your hands in your pockets

and your shirtail OUT

II.
that little boy
slinking his arm
into the long silky glove
puts the pole between his legs
and rides his cock horse
to bamberry cross
on the royal glass mountain
in the basement
his high black hard shiny custom riding boots
and breeches of softest chamois
draining stares from passersby
he is stupefied with power

III.
Joyriding one night
he gets stuck in a ditch
can't go home
lights out for the Y
stupefied with shame

IV.
The two professionals arrive
to perform their undertaking
with appropriate solemnity
the Latin guy is young
an apprentice in the business

they go upstairs
the three of us wait
benumbed and averse
to observing their labors
three bodies descend the stairs
hers in the bag
the gurney exits
he howls and howls
a sound heard maybe
by someone next door
of someone being tortured

V.
We sat on the foot of the bed
it was 4 AM
I was cold
"Do you mind if I close the window?"
He, rather than I
moved toward it, explaining
"She always needed a flow of air"
it was ok to close it:
the you-name-it had left

At that precise moment
I had to slam
that cultural baggage
shut

VI.
He lost no time
courted the first skirt

enacted in quick relief
a synopsis of need
drank liters of Dekuyper
cherry flavored brandy
flooded the house
clung to the cat
mollified his daughter
sat
alone
in groups
alone in groups
talked
and talked
played Schubert's Trio in B flat major
wept
howled
the year passed

VII.
Fingers thickened and stiffened
he unpacks his clarinet
embouchure gone
along with her lungs
Mozart staggers
"Grandpa, what's a priest?"
jolted to the real
of the uninjured child
"A priest is someone. . .
who speaks for God"
"That can't be true

he must be guessing"
back in the saddle. . .
something relents

VIII.
That war-torn face
those futile tics
and hunkered frame
what a puzzle
that we begin
in parents' abandon
ancient passions
and all that
a thing apart
his thoughtless life
did not evolve
from others' primal joys

IX.
A sister's dispassion
masking anger with reason
the burden of knowledge
our cards ever stacked
glib with his secrets
somewhere in it
a vengeful shedding
Sebastian, Jeckyl, Wilde, and Hyde
the rubrics of wisdom
depth, uniqueness

sacrifice, love,
Rousseau's goodness

dignity stifles
the working man
who seeks redemption's
wily cure
and nothing less
than exorcism
if only
if not

pity
can be taught
can compassion?

Ladies Who Lunch

The shop oozes with exotica
diaphanous, spangled, draped, flung
hardly room to move
the proprietor, her pale face
clowned with aqua
flutters over her dishabille domain
two large dark West Indian women
confident shoppers
who know what they want
roam the aisles
without success

Clown lady, agitated
"This is beeootiful
try it on. . .no I don't have
large sizes"
I chime in "You know
I was in Bloomingdale's
the other day
they had some lovely things
in larger sizes
I wished they could fit me"
"Yes I know Bloomingdale's
I got this in Bloomingdale's
I want something transparent"
Ah

Still they persist
surely under the next pile...

clown lady suddenly
cannot contain herself
"What do you want from me
what do you want from me?!"
she has changed the name of the game
from shopping to the unspeakable
"What did you say?...
(pursuing the proprietor
who flees down the aisle)
I heard what you said"
"Try this on, it will go with your blouse"
"No, you can't sweet-talk us now
what did you mean?
you should learn something
just because our skin

Labor Day Faces

The negotiations
around I am not you
become moot
at parting

a moue on one face
Keaton on the other

each wave of feeling
still roiled
from household dithering

but at this disjuncture
we know what's what

For George Sugarman

You lived alone one floor up
loftbed, stove
ladder, old square desk
two-by-fours, C-clamps
and wooden things
sanded, glued, sanded again
suddenly one day
they explode
blue! red! yellow!

You ate your frenchbread and cheese
on newspaper
spread over the desk
tore out the middle
(which this visitor nibbled)
preferring the crust
sucked on your cigarettes
and inky coffee
the aluminum pot
day-long ready

Maybe you loved me
it was hard to tell
the daily work
was everything
that's what I loved
that was my school
the ominous things
eluded the syllabus

intimations
doubts, shoals
melodramas
nipped in the bud
given short shrift
Making Art
was the only measure

"I could kick off at any time"
undramatically delivered
over Walker's soup
growling and grinning
you looked at me squarely
defying response

Grieving for you
I grieve for that girl
who climbed your stairs
and nibbled your bread
who thought she could live
your monk-like devotion
without repercussion
I hear your dry snort
"SO. . . that's the story"

Macaronics

Narrative needs
a verb to proceed
poetry courts the noun
forget all the adjectives
turned upside down

Gerunds unite
while adverbs clamor
for representation
in the general glamour

Forego all the clutter
squished by compression
let us all revel
in meaning's expansion

Sometimes, however
I am called to action
by the siren song
of that narrative faction

Endgames

They're dropping like flies
George and Dick
Nancy and Al
Sugarman, Bellamy
Topf and Taylor
even Moondog finally
and now Rudy

The obits keep coming
retched up from the files

Watch us habitués
of all the news
that's fit to print
turn first to the
C Section
there but for the grace. . .
the alleged departed
loom more real in print
than in former absentia

Breakfast of Champions

The great ones assemble
grown old they dissemble
hide their shock at the wrinkles
in awed recognition
"Down with the chins"
prompts the photographer
"Which ones?" quips the sculptor

Another flouts custom
puts his ass in the air
later we stare
"I know you" I blare
We're here all together
minus kidneys and breasts
former philanderers
now dowager queens
embattled transgressors
now chastened and lean
survivors of trauma
and cultural wars
hoarding our victories
concealing our sores

To all of these champions
I offer a toast
from here to eternity
we've only to coast

Walking in the City

I can still love this time of day
east from Chelsea
south to St. Marks
a toothless moon
clearing the autumnal towers
each aglow in the sun's spent light

As long as I can pass tattoo parlors
palm readers, Greek luncheonettes, bodegas
there may still be room to breathe
in this devouring town

Keep moving

Indices

The impression of your head
etches the pillow
like Belle's
after those guys
took her body away

Your dreams pool
in the template linen
my words clog
the computer's cogs

I patrol this space
like the absent cat
once scoured for traces

my vanished mouse

December 28, 1999 Flamingo Lodge, FL

The heavy air
the shrill call
the unseen bird
the piercing reeds

I am as heavy
with foreboding
impervious to the light
as the sound
of one palm frond scraping

"Oh, that's just another pelican"

Thoreau said
"If I could,
I would worship
the parings of my nails."

The Fly

On my minuscule balcony
in the Melbourne, FL Hilton
across the road
from acres of Airstreams
sprawled like glittering slugs
torpid in the tropical air

I watch the death throes of the fly
I have just brushed from my arm

Have I put you out of your misery?
put an end to your sorrows?
relieved you of the nuisance of living?

Berlin -- August 2000

reading

Vienna 1900

thinking

New York 1960-2000

seeing

Judisches Museum

      empty shell
      overflowing
      a tower
      a door

hearing
      that sound
      as it swings shut

All ye who enter here...

These Rummy Times

Ugh that leer
that comes and goes
with no relation
to what he knows

A slickish tick
betrays his glee
"I'm having the time of my life
pay attention to me"

<u>His</u> intelligence tells him
unspeakable things
which he then metes out
on unflappable wings

<u>Our</u> intelligence wavers
as we listen to him
caught between mouthfuls
and the general din

The World Upside Down

When does the sky look like the sea
and the sea look like the sky?
The world turned upside down
The sky a vast abyss
The sea a burning cosmos
      waging peace
      keeping war
The language belongs to the liars

Where's the compassion?
Depends on what you mean by "where's"

December 24, 2010

Rule of Thumb:
when the partner cries
embrace her
hang on for dear life

Tides

I miss you today
my eyes well up
with your nearness

Will you think of me
on the eve
of <u>your</u> homecoming?

At the end of this day
the city still surging
I try to remember you

A casualness
suffusing your voice
your nervous laugh
my body tenses
like a stone dropping

I ride your tides
like a reckless surfer
waiting to crash
in the shallows' calm
I dream of arrival

The train's rhythmic rocking
lulling south the flaming trees
pangs of anticipation
already prefigure
the stifling of desire

We toe our past constraints
while nature flares around us
in this burst of longing
tethered, yet adrift

Four days later
tearing south at 70mph
unsaid, unsung, unstrung
I catch the train home
with ten seconds to spare

Untitled

A 90-year-old woman
walks 3,000 miles
for campaign contribution reform

A 6-year-old boy
shoots a 6-year-old girl
dead

One of them
maybe two
will never look back